More Than Enough

An Anthology from

The Sacramento Poetry Center

Writing Groups

Published by

SPC Press
The Sacramento Poetry Center
1719 25th Street
Sacramento, CA 95816

In Cooperation with

Inner Works Press
103 Ellis Ave
Normal, IL 61761

More Than Enough
Table Of Contents

I

*Poem titles with asterisks were previously published elsewhere.

A Word From The SPC President

Poets need community, and The Community needs poets. If I learned anything about poets, poetry, and poetry centers over these years of being the Sacramento Poetry Center's (SPC) pandemic president, it's that their chief business is community. It's not that poets don't need to hone their craft, or that the ancient tradition of poetry isn't a noble enough pursuit on its own; but rather, what I've seen people asking for, fighting for, and yearning for, is community. I've also seen our world turn to poets, on the big stage, and a small stage, from The White House, to a living room. The Community needs the thoughts and words of our poets.

This collection is one of the Center's greatest achievements. Not because it's a new publication, or because voices are given a platform, or because books matter. This collection is special, because it is the distillation of a community that weathered a storm together, sometimes in pain, sometimes in joy. These are our words, broken as bread between us, when nothing else would sustain. And now, they are your words, words to feed a whole community. Take them and pass them around. There's more than enough.

Stuart Canton, President
Sacramento Poetry Center
May 2022

Preface

For many of us, writing poetry is a doorway to a world of expression that connects us to a deeper current of life. The evocative nature of poetry taps into one's memories, emotions, imagination, and personal history. In poetry, the condensed language, the use of metaphor, the shape and sound of words, the metered rhythms, and poetic structures serve many purposes - not only in imparting meaning but in expressing and creating an experience. In writing poetry, we open a line of communication that flows, like a river that goes beyond ourselves and takes us on a journey to a world of possibilities outside of our own frames of reference. Once we drink from that deeper current, it is easy to get hooked.

When the pandemic hit, it was a perfect opportunity to write in earnest. Seasoned and novice poets suddenly had more time to devote to writing. The Sacramento Poetry Center (SPC) already offered two well-established writing groups that met weekly: the long-running Tuesday Night Workshop facilitated by Danyen Powell and the more recent Marie Writers Prompt Writing workshop facilitated by Bob Stanley. The pandemic spawned two more weekly writing groups: Writing From The Inside Out Prompt Writing, which I facilitate; and the Coast To Coast Poetry Consortium facilitated by Len Germinara. As the pandemic dragged on, these weekly groups kept meeting and members were producing a good deal of fine poetry. It was, therefore, only natural to propose publishing an anthology of participants' poems. This collection is the result.

I took the lead on the project along with a committee comprised of Angela James, Ann Michaels, and Len Germinara. We thought it may be helpful for readers to understand how the book is organized in order to get the most out of it. The book is organized into four main sections, by writing group and according to its longevity. The Introduction to each section, written by the respective group leaders, includes a brief history and describes the group's purpose, process and format. The title, *More Than Enough,* honors Andru Defeye, current poet laureate of Sacramento and whose poem, "Enough," is included as the first poem in the collection. It is a beautiful and touching poem that addresses the sense of inadequacy, that feeling of not being enough, that plagues so many of us in life despite our talents and accomplishments. The title, *More Than Enough,* is meant to be inclusive of all the authors and poems that make up this anthology.

As an anthology, the poems in the collection do not necessarily follow a consistent theme or address a common topic. The table of contents displays both the poem title and its author in alphabetical order by author last name with the exception of Andru Defeye's poem, as mentioned above, which was submitted to the Coast To Coast Poetry Consortium group. We also accepted one longer poem that exceeded our line count: Susan Wolbert's poem in honor of Sacramento poet Jim Moose.

It was a joy to work with Angela, Ann, and Len in producing this book. We are proud to share the work of those who have participated in Sacramento Poetry Center's writing groups. Hopefully, this collection highlights the benefits of a writing community, both to hone one's own work and to support and encourage others to write. If any poem in this collection gives you a taste of the deeper current, or touches you in some way, and especially if it inspires you to write, it has done *more than enough* to fulfill its purpose.

Nick LeForce
April 2022

More Than Enough

Introduction

The Sacramento Poetry Center was founded in 1979 to provide a place for poets to read, write, and share their work. Today, 43 years later, SPC still fulfills that mission. Laverne Frith ran the Tuesday night workshop for over a decade, and sadly, Laverne and his wife Carol, both fine poets and group leaders, passed away in 2020. They were the consummate poets – serious and dedicated and connected, kind and careful practitioners who wrote and published and helped others do the same. Danyen Powell stepped in, and for over two decades, he has continued to follow the precepts of the Friths – making sure that everyone gets their turn and gets a supportive, but honest critique in 90 minutes of intensity on Tuesday nights. This group – I'm sure it's at least 30 years old – continues to flourish, and many successful poets trace their early inspirations to the Tuesday night workshop.

Writing groups – free and accessible writing groups – are an important part of any community, whether the goal is literary excellence or unedited free expression. Over the past 30 years, Sacramento has had a wealth of excellent groups for people to express themselves and work on their craft. Thanks to SutterWriters and Escritores del Nuevo Sol, SPC's Tuesday Night Workshop, and Jan Haag's Soul of the Narrator group, writers have been able to gather, either online or in person, and write, critique, revise; and then – in the inimitable way of the poet, to do it all over again. For young people, organizations like 916INK and SAYS provide this important service. We're lucky to have so many people in Sacramento writing in so many groups in our region, and that's a testimonial to the organizations and people who volunteer to keep these groups going.

The Covid-19 pandemic, with all its upheaval to our social order, moved writing circles (along with everything else) into the online arena. Some people wrote *more* during our quarantine years, which speaks to the power of the activity – writing in itself. I'm guessing that much of the work in this collection was written in 2020 and 2021. The leaders of the various groups kept things going and provided needed space for writers. Why we write may differ, but we all have found some nourishment in the process of writing. The poems here are evidence of that nourishment, that shared table.

I was glad to hear from Ann Michaels and Nick LeForce when they offered to put together this anthology of the poets and writers who attend the current slate of workshops that SPC organizes. A successful poetry community needs to celebrate new writers and honor people who write because they want to, because they need to. Every week I learn from the other writers in our group; we're all learners here. This is an anthology of work by dedicated writers; some of us are in print for the first time. I hope that you, the readers of this anthology will be touched by at least a poem or two, and I hope you'll let the writers of those poems know what touched you. We write to connect. Only the reader can complete the loop by writing back.

Please enjoy this anthology of Sacramento writers!

Bob Stanley,
March 2022

More Than Enough

Andru Defeye – Enough

You are enough

Divinity flows in your fingertips
        with light so radiant
        every beat of your heart
a victory march
made of whole universes
        stitched by the hands of creation
        with flawless design
a prophecy You fulfill perfectly with every breath

        You

The sun wouldn't shine the same without it
Creation is only waiting for You
                to smile back at it

Do you see it yet?

You are enough
        For the birds to sing about
        For the seeds to sprout about
        For the stars to shoot about

        Do you see it yet?

        Gardens in your speech
Fields of wildflowers in your prayers
        Lighthouses in your eyes
        No one else can see it for you

You have always been enough
You will always be enough

Your simple act of being is enough

        Do you see it yet?

Tuesday Night Workshop

The Sacramento Poetry Center has been hosting a Tuesday night poetry workshop for over 30 years. And it's still going strong. Hosted/facilitated by Danyen Powell, it's both in person (at the Sacramento Poetry Center) and on Zoom. Participants range in age from 12 to 97 years old.

Process & Format

This workshop can be very useful for those serious about developing and publishing their work. Poets get constructive feedback from other poets on poems they have written. The workshop begins promptly at 7:30pm and ends at 9pm. The facilitator calls on people to share their poem, either on screen or by distributed copy, and the author reads it aloud. The group gives constructive feedback and the author silently listens. Once the critique is complete, the facilitator invites the author to ask any clarifying questions or make brief comments. Due to time constraints, poems should be one page (8 1/2 X 11) in 12 font. Poems are not workshopped over email or between sessions.

How to access the group:

Newcomers are welcome to audit the workshop without bringing a poem the first time to get a feel for it. You can participate in the workshop by emailing your poem to: sac.tuesday.poetry@gmail.com by 6:30 pm Tuesday so all the poems are screen-shared from one place.

Facilitated by Danyen Powell

Maxine Boshes – Recovery

When the anesthetic fades
and the healing has begun
that's when the pain sets in—
when you've barely stopped, you run

So you look around your room
then you look around your soul
til you see well all those things
you've not looked at until now

Now that hope can shine its light
you can't hide inside the night
With the healing medicine
well, that's when the pain sets in

When you start to mend a chair
you will see the broken stair—
oh, much easier is flight
and that hiding in the night

Now that anesthetic's gone
and you can't get rid of hope
you can't take off and run cause
now's when the pain sets in

So you see the course just run
And the unmarked road ahead
you've only just begun to
keep fear from setting in

Then one morning filled with sun
you begin to run because it's fun
So sweet to feel such joy when
recovery has begun

Vicki Carroll – Here I am

waiting for inspiration
wondering if thoughts will come
So far, I am feeling pretty dumb

I wait for progress, nothing yet
I wait and wonder and here I set

Nothing spectacular coming to me
Wishing and hoping I will see
a nice little hook or great little rhyme
to get everyone laughing just in time

Can creativity get caught
  between the head and the hand
    with so much pressure
      to exceed my demand?

I wait for progress, nothing yet
I wait and wonder and here I set

Seems so, on this fine day
as I write and write
with nothing fabulous to say
wishing and hoping this block goes away

No mind shattering truths
or even a pretty phrase
rattling around my silly old brain
So, I set my sights on some
incredible refrain

I wait for progress, nothing yet
I wait and wonder and here I set

Karen DeFoe – Mourning in Winter*

For Francesco and Will

The frigid hand of winter has begun
To paint the sky in steely shades of gray
And dim the light and warmth of autumn's sun
To lengthen hours of darkness in the day.
While Boreas exhales his icy breath,
And bends the boughs that shake against the cold,
The frost from naughty Jack brings sudden death
To comely flowers I could once behold.
A melancholy madness may portend
The rolling fog - the sleet - the freezing snow,
But I, with April heart, do not intend
To dwell on winter's darkness or its woe.
      For frost will thaw and bluebirds soon will sing,
      As light returns and new life blooms in spring.

*Previously published in *Ink Spots: Award-winning Flash Fiction & Poetry* (2022 Gold Country Writers Press)

M. J. Donovan – Crows*

circle over C Street Park at dusk
a cacophony undulating
on air currents until they find a roost

only to reappear at dawn
a start of wings and hollers
scattering across the city morning

five land on Mrs. Guzman's roof
seven stride over Mr. Mah's lawn
one hundred and three fly east toward River Park

all day they inspect, peck, pester the mockingbirds
eat worms, walnuts, abandoned burritos
until dusk pulls them back

a cantankerous cloud
settling into twilight bickering
in the sycamore by the railway tracks

the same place they escape the storms
feathers frazzled, slicked with rain

*Previously published on estreetpost.com

Nancy Ginsberg – Springtime Along The Delta

Springtime is upon us!
Barren trees transforming into
delicate buds of pink and white blossoms.
Waiting for the blooming time to be viewed -
from the scenic banks by their reflections,
of colorful beauty - as seen upon the still
waterways of the delta.

Joan Goodreau – Masks

Evacuate again
my autistic son and me.

Not the Paradise Fire this time
another fire chases us and
Corona follows wherever we go.

I see you
through a mask of smoke
the outlines of your life
blurred hazy
remember you so small
a dark mystery I could not solve.

I see you
in a mask of cloth
can't see you grin or
hear your whispered words
remember you so small
before you had sounds or smiles.

We carry on our way like always
but still hide smiles and muffled words
behind our masks.

Wander through smoke
wonder where to next?

Tom Hedt – Succession

We have a string of diesel
locomotives in town -
patient, rusting, majestic
in their idle. It's been over

twenty years since the tracks
through the Eel River canyon blew
out and left them behind. Now the relics
are kept in a weedy tract, confined
by a chain link fence. People pass
by, never paying much attention.

It can be that way with old things.
Sitting in the simple dignity
of stranded circumstance. Echoing
the grandeur of rusted dreams
that once transformed the world.

Gary Kruse – While Thinking of Charles Simic...

...I Remember The Fox

A fox made a home for himself in a cabinet below our sink in the kitchen. He'd let himself out once we'd all hit the sack. He'd slide down the hall to the living room. And there he'd be washed in the blue glow of the nightlights at the base of the walls, shadowed by what pulsed through the curtains from a streetlamp. And once in the room, he'd always waltz. He'd glide about between the sofa and chairs, so gracefully, beside an unseen partner, with his fine tail swishing this way and that. He'd hum an old tune in a low nasal whine as only a fox can do.

But when that fox died of old age, Dad took to the sauce. A few times a week we heard him, as he broke out in curses—Old English curses in the middle of the night. Said he heard the fox when it nudged a vase or tipped a lamp. We explained again and again that the fox had died but to no avail. And from that time on, life at home was never the same.

Sharon Mahany – Holding Anchor

Light falls on paths we have come to know
    Wind rips memories across our faces
        eyes shut tight to block the burn

Hair whips sand into strident meteors
scattering like stars atop the glittering surf

We dance in visions of time
melding heartbeats with crashing waves

Search for our feet under tumultuous depths
not knowing what monster we might find

It is along the coast we find a dull gray of sky
veiling past from future

holding anchor between shipwreck and sun
wave and sand, our souls one

It is here at the edge of waves
    we build castles, fill into form
        light and shadow   then story our dream

Reneé Marie – Truth-Be-Told

An ax splits wood
for a cold hungry stove

A pen splits reality
for a past, a present, a story still
untold and I

dream there is always enough wood and

> *would you please me*
> *with your warm loving company*
> *would you pencil-me-in to all your tomorrows*
> *with a softness I can only imagine*

Is there enough wood for the body's hunger here
Are there enough pens for the secrets we tell
ourselves and sharpened pencils for drawing
our dreams, alive?

I crave there is always enough
       kindling
       wedges
       shims

       Papermate
       Pentel
       Cross.

       Pilot me safely home
       split me open
       ablaze
       in our warming
       story.

Matthew Mitchell – Witness

(Reflections on a Sacramento Bee photograph of several mourners at the
gravesite of Stephon Clark)

Then came the cops
with five quick shots

and six months on
a serious few

still bear witness
in greensward

of south cemetery
standing up straight

in grass that may have filled
the man killed

with fear of death just like mine
whenever he drove by

fear of ending
down here

in South Sac
below a marble rectangle

flat to floodplain
under brown summer skies

insensate to people like me
driving distracted

blind to the circumferences
he faced

imagining ourselves outside them
bound for elsewhere

Shawn Pittard – Shelter In Place

How normal the day. The alarm singing,
as always, at 5:05 am. The easing about
to relieve the chronic pains. Moving damp
clothes from the washer to the dryer.
Grinding coffee beans. Bringing water
almost to a boil. There is a cool shade
of a breeze on the patio. The succulents
are tidy in their southwestern planters. I know
why Adam ate the apple. Why Cain killed Abel.

Betsy (Sunderland) Powell – In Revloc

He left for work in the dark,
a coal-patch, ten-street, company town
courtesy of the Coleman and Weaver Mining Company.

Black smudges still showed
on his freshly washed clothes
as he silently trudged to Mine #32.

He passed the supply hoist and the dynamite shed
with his lunch bucket, pick and headlamp in hand
descending hundreds of feet.

Lying on his stomach in the gently suffocating air,
he covered his burning coughs with a clenched fist
while filling the coal car twice a day.

Quitting was not an option—he owed the Company his life.
The next generation of miners would be his sons.

Their inheritance would be the poor pay
and working conditions.
He had to make changes—a strike!

In a church basement he led the secret meetings;
the word got out
Company Police scoured the streets.

Curfews, beatings, threats of evictions...
The coal miners won!
Then a doctor's visit identified black lung—

Two months later he was buried in the Company graveyard.
His last words to his sons:
I am the final payment to this Company town.

Danyen Powell – The Tree Of Centuries Lost

its trunk scarred
        by the endless epitaphs
of our words
         bleeding sap

its roots searching
        for the heartbeat
of ancient cities
        stacked under our feet

        *

the swing under its canopy
is for all of us

our bodies gliding
        over the vast
emptiness beneath us

our shadows flung out
        across the world

Marilynn Price – Astronaut

you are gravity
    when gravity is gone

the pouch of yourself
    in a foil suit

orbiting in a vacuum
        the air pocket of home

a blue pearl in a windowpane

Allegra Jostad Silberstein – Field of Light

(a poem inspired by Chella's painting at the Natsoulas: 2020)

Light streams down
through the trees to the path
curving around them
beckoning me . . .
an invitation.

An alder on the edge
smaller with bent trunk
speaks to me
without words or sound.
We are one in a field of light.

Susan Wolbarst – Visiting Jim Moose

Since you told me not to visit you,
because you don't want to share your sickness
I visit you in my imagination.
I stand beside you on the ship's deck
in the pouring rain, admiring
your Napoleonic garb, complete with bicorne,
as our craft thwack thwack thwacks on the chop.
Your poet brain makes a mental note that
when describing this scene later,
the term "tempest-tossed" (you might even go for tost)
would be appropriate.

I sit quietly in the back of your courtroom
listening to the lawyers go on and on, the people this
and the people that, and respondent's hired gun fingering
his silk tie and saying things like "I demur."
Both sides are your honoring the heck out of you,
but you seem piqued by the total lack of logic on display
in a chamber amply filled with conjecture, even fantasy.
After everyone has gone, I approach the bench,
and we have a brief conversation. You, distracted by your work,
leave for your office. Beneath your black robe,
I see you are wearing red Converse high-tops.

You say, using the popular vernacular, "let's grab a cup of coffee."
I say, "I know just the place." I fill my heavy pale green Stanley thermos
with strong brew and take you to Guincho Beach. No sanitized coffee bar
here,
just the sea, the beach littered with cuttlefish skeletons
ready for parakeet cages on some other continent,
and a crumbling fort from the 1600s, which I know you will appreciate.
I pour your coffee into the silver thermos lid,
and mine into the paper Starbucks cup I have brought along for irony,
and get ready to reveal something about this favorite place.
But before I can do it, you say, 'this is the westernmost point in Europe,"
saying exactly what I had planned to tell you.
I should have known that you would know that.
You smile, and I wonder what is left to say about this place,
whether I should tell you that guincho means "squeal" in Portuguese,

named after the eerie sound made by wind and groups of rocks
holding on to the ocean as it pulls away from them,
moving even further west.

Arlene Downing-Yaconelli – rain

plumb lines of diamond drops
hang to earth and   fracture
sunshine to color

cool sprizzles of mist
swaddle the air and diffuse
light to whispered hues

wind-driven needles
slashed by white flashes melt
electric through haloed coronas

at times
the liquid drift
floats gently
caught and held
by rising currents of air
just long enough to defy earth's pull
past startled eyes
then sinks   slides-----------
into collars   over boot tops
around umbrellas
drops chortle and gather
and fall on dampened heads

chilled   chafed   wet and blinded

ah, but the rainbows!

Marie Writers

Marie Writers was founded in honor of Marie Reynolds, a wonderful poet whom I was fortunate to know. Marie was active in many writing groups in Sacramento, especially the vibrant group led by Jan Haag that uses the Amherst (AWA) approach to creative writing. Before Marie died of breast cancer in fall 2018, she made a generous contribution to SPC. I told her we'd start a weekly writing group in her name, and she loved the idea. The group, with some variation, has been meeting steadily for the last 3 1/2 years.

Process & Format

Loosely modeled on the AWA method, MarieWriters is a generative work-shop – participants share leading the group and providing prompts. We write for about 30 minutes and we give only positive feedback – looking for strengths in the writing – for another 45 minutes or so. We meet Wednesday nights from 6 to 7:30, and welcome new writers! Since 2020, we've been online, we plan to stay that way – it gets more people in-volved. I've learned a lot from the other writers in the group, and it's great for me to see their work in this collection.

How to Access This Group:

Interested writers can access this group through the Sacramento Poetry Center website: www.sacpoetrycenter.org

Facilitated by Bob Stanley

Note: If you want to get to know Marie Reynolds, you can get her book of poems, *Seaworthy*, which was published before she passed away, by River Rock Press. It's a good one.

Julie Hannah Brower – The Black-Blue of Perfection

night arrives
into a nest of twigs
two birds
three birds
five birds
feathered wings
tipped by red
home the size of a car tire
cotton, lint, mudded leaves fill the tracks
restless as dark settles
then quiet
high enough above ground to avoid becoming prey
murmurs
almost as a dog asleep
sound rattles through their throats
beaks softly grate
top against bottom

the sky
its own black-blue
studded with stars
leather-jacketed gay men from the seventies, eighties
how many dead now
bodies bruised
lesions
spirits adrift
or finally tethered
go
don't go
go now

we'll all go
become the black-blue speed
that spins forever
feathered
studded
trajectory unknown
then morning
then morning

Lesley Cummings – The Well

I am resting
On the wall of an old well.
I am far
down, close to the surface
of the water.
The circle of light
at the top
is the size of a nickel.

The quiet throbs.
It is twilight here.

A small swirl appears and
twists on the water's surface.

The swirl grows bigger.
and bigger still.
Small waves hit the wall.
I am hypnotized
by the swirling and the splashing.

Through the swirl,
dandelions of light
begin to poke through.
Each has a tiny sound of its own.

First a few,
then hundreds
then thousands
The well is filled
with harmony and light.

The dandelions flow through me.
Each one warms me,
lightens me,
eases my heart.

I feel found.

Diane Funston – In The Garden

In the garden
surrounded by orchards
and rice fields
we planted lemons, oranges, pomegranates and grapes
with enough foliage to shelter us
from the reality of city living.

Shrubs grew high
vines entwined,
we grew poetry in with petunias
picked words from the cauliflower
untangled good lines
from night-blooming jasmine.

You said "Carve me and you inside a heart
on a tree, we have plenty".
I said, "Cleave onto me
in the bushes under cover of twilight".

We embraced and became one
between the redwood tree
and the mission fig.
We have marked this place as ours
deep in foliage that shelters us
from our reality of city living.

Nick LeForce – Aimless Love

Aimless love took my fickle heart
by default, hitched it to the everyday,
leashed it to joy, insisting
I take a walk in the world
and bless the early buds
on barren branches, shaking
their booty in the wind;

that I feel the way my feet
mold to the ground with each step
as if it is a homecoming;

that I take this dear blue sky
as my companion and confess
all the ways I have fallen from grace
neglecting its all consuming delight;

that I shine this silly something-
up-the-sleeve grin through
my unmasked eyes, aiming
this aimless love at you,
infecting your fickle heart
with viral affections
that unleash this
inexplicable joy
on the world.

Valerie Ries-Lerman – Living Now

Breathe as if it's your last breath.
Walk a road untended and wild.
Pay attention to the details that sketch your life,
draw bold and wide, ignoring mediocrity.

Honor the love that binds.
Be present for the small gifts laid upon your table;
for your spirit to open, soul to unwind.
Become one with all we share:
world connected, sublime.

Laura Martin — The House On North 5th Street

Don't worry for now
about the bones of this
100-year-old house—
good and sturdy
they have propped themselves
up for all these years
no matter the creaks and squeaks
the unevenness of floors
the slight detachment of ceiling from wall
the paint that peels back tenderly
like sunburnt skin

Standing strong this house has
through two World Wars
(and all the wars after)
through fire, heavy rains and earthquake
through cityscape uprising around it
even through unspeakable heartache
of death and departure
it stood a safe shelter
for multitudes of grieving,
the smell of your mother's pozole
penetrating every room

And look, here, through the back window
your father's abundant garden of a yard—
the guava and persimmons,
the passion fruit and
Oklahoma turtles hiding asleep for winter,
the pomegranate tree
he planted decades ago—
dug the earth with his own hands
unfurled the root ball to fit into this tiny pit of earth
so you would always have something sweet,
and roots so deep now in the dirt
untraceable in every direction

Ann Michaels – Communing with Giants

For my sister, Kristine

What do you want me to tell you?

I asked the small giant under the warm cover of night.

Its thick cinnamon-colored bark as large as my palms,
its branches end in deep green
its needles used as cushion for long sitting and contemplation.

With my eyes closed, I whisper a story
about a little brown girl who grew up
riding waves near the edges of the earth,
she climbs tall trees,
befriends mountains and
sings love songs to the moon.

She had small hands for large giving,
a heart for loving as vast as the sky
and her laughs emit a sound as if
fairies sprinkled joy in the air.

I tell the small giant:

Sometimes, I wish I were this girl,
with all her magic and light and belief in the world.

Sometimes, I think I could be this girl
and I aspire to try
and imagine
a self who breathes the joy in
and the joy out.

Sometimes, I go to the ocean.

Sometimes, I am she,
sitting under a canopy of stars
exhaling joy,
while singing her love song to the moon.

David Quinley – Two Short Poems

Untitled

To come out the other end
You must 1st enter

At a Distance

Seeking
The earliest of memories
Like trying to hear an echo
Long since passed

Kris Robinson – Love is

like discovering
          a forgotten
               banknote
wadded-up
      in a thrift store

   pocket,
      sometimes,
  found in
             the long wait

for a table,

Friday nights

  at Musso & Frank, or
briefly seen in

    a discarded photo,
          tossed and
          tumbling down

    a windy street,

perhaps, found in
    the director's cut,

    now available

for same-day delivery;

   but often,
       such things

    are best left
      simply as

               deleted scenes.

Laura Rosenthal – Hidden*

Beneath girl's translucent skin,
crone lurks.

*Previously Published in *Brevities* and in *Sacramento Voices 2018* (Cold River Press)

Bob Stanley – Weaving the light

In memoriam Rod Rhines, 1972-2018

Standing silent on the long wooden pier,
I stood in moonlight on the lake and thought of you,
light from a hundred wave-crests filling my eyes.

With the roundness of the moon and the softness of wind
across the water, remembering you is both easy and hard,
for we walked through this same moonlight a decade ago.

Always preparing in the way one must prepare,
you loved those around you with a starry gleam,
each day reaching for whatever fullness time would allow.

I call out to reach you now, illuminated for a moment,
Trying to weave a tapestry of darkness and light,
some continuing dance of earth and water and moon and you.

Patricia Wentzel – Mr. Tamaguchi

In my junior year of high school Stateside—
Inclined to rebellion but given no choice—
I showed up for Biology determined to be bored
Slumped into a desk, into the plastic attached seat
Fingered the sharp edge of my hard-backed binder
Stared unseeing at the blackboard

You were shorter than me
Spry, black-haired, smiled a lot
My face felt stiff and unused when I half-smiled back

You made Biology interesting
Maybe it was your commitment to making accurate
Detailed information about the human reproductive system
Relevant, accessible
I was grateful for those lessons later
During my wild days in Long Beach

When you turned to Mendelian inheritance
Investigations into the color of Sweat Peas
My curiosity kicked in
Despite my mutinous inclinations
Resentful learner mutated into eager disciple

You congratulated me at Graduation
It meant a lot to me
The only teacher that sought me out
The only teacher whose name I still recall

Writing From The Inside Out

In April 2020, I created an online writing workshop, Writing From the Inside Out, to help fill the Covid gap by offering writing prompts and a platform for new and experienced poets to share their work. The purpose is to encourage and stimulate new writing and offer a platform to give each other positive feedback and encouragement for our writing.

Process and Format

Each Monday, I send out an email to registered participants with a selected poem, a paragraph or two of my thoughts about the poem, and a set of writing prompts to stimulate creativity and inspire writing. Anyone is welcome to register and receive the weekly prompts. All registrants are also invited to share their writing by joining a "read-around" on Thursday afternoons. We generally follow the Amherst Writer's and Artists method for giving feedback by offering supportive comments about what we think is strong in the poem, point out particular lines or stanzas we enjoy and note how the poem impacts us. Sharing a poem is not required and some occasionally come simply to listen.

How To Access This Group:

To register, got to www.sacpoetrycenter.org and select writing from the inside out on the home page or go to www.nickleforce.com → Inside Out to read the most recent prompts online.

Facilitated by Nick LeForce

Beth Bartel – Your headline here

Your headline here

In local news today, an unidentified woman was found
pacing the intersection of Burnout and Balance

Traffic was heavily congested due to passersby rubbernecking
Because People Can't Mind Their Own Business

After about an hour, the woman, still not saying a word about
who she was, where she was trying to go, or how she planned to get there
left and headed toward the intersection of Confusion and Clarity

As she carefully navigated her way down the Existential Expressway, she was confronted by
horn-blowing, obscenity-yelling, and finger-flipping
by those who were in much more of a hurry to get to the same destination

In related news, a referendum to affirm every citizen's God-given right to
free speech in matters concerning telling others how to run their lives is
gaining traction with the town council

More on this on tonight's special broadcast after the 11:00 news
"Yes, You Can and Should Be All Up in Their Business"
sponsored by Winkerton Security Cameras and the Winkerton App
available for download in your app store

Now for the weather

Doreen Beyer – Gift of a Day

The old woman stood facing east,
on the shore of a serpentine path,
like a tiny tree
leaning into a metal walker—
little waves of people, like me,
drift by—walking dogs.

She stood to witness the birth
of a new day, her eyes shimmering
with the vision of an orange
glow on the horizon,
opening the landscape—
lighting her face.

Turning stiffly at my approach,
her pale, watery eyes iridesce words
summoned from wonderment—
isn't this beautiful?
Slowly, her gaze returns to the
distant glow.

Memory has erased her face,
but I will remember my polite pause,
the force of her appreciation,
and my eventual failure to fight
against the hurry, hurry,
hurrying past—
outside of the ticking moment.

Vicki Carroll – Everything Aligns

I am here living my dream
Please stop by and we can visit
      have a treat together
Tell some stories, laugh
      and keep these memories close

Somehow, we know it is time to count
      our blessings   look into the eyes
of the eternal watchers see their ongoing
      expressions to know how our works
are in line with our hopes and dreams

Can we keep our faith in what cannot be seen
      until we transition into our next assignment?
Let's carry on, that is what we do— "Carry On"
      there is no beginning or end

Eternity never ends
      compartmentalization
      our only separation

Gene Cheever – The Sun

Some say the sun
Is predictable

It will rise in the morning
And set in the evening

It will rise in the east
And set in the west

It will have a summer solstice
And a winter solstice

....

Others say yes
But consider

When it rises
It might hide behind clouds

When it dresses
It might wear yellow orange or red

When it floats
It might grow or shrink

And when it sets
It might paint a beautiful landscape
Laced with cloud and color like no other

Sue Daly – Regret

is a bitter
mirror.

Drop it.
Let it shatter –

splinter
into shards
at your feet.

Walk away –
don't look back.

Susan Dlugach – A Dance

The sunfed spring wind is teasing
a fulsome oak over the fence,
ruffling her apple green branches.
Her newly bloomed dress
cha cha chas as she chitters
in tree laughter,
her lover's attention welcome
this blue sky day birthing
a season of lust, love and seed
before falling under a different wind,
an opposite wind,
a harsher lover
who strips her down
leaving naked her limbs,
her skeletal self a stark figure
against a darkening sky,
yet still she shelters wingéd ones
and ones who whisk away
what she leaves to nurture them
til spring returns.

Diane Funston – Kumquats

Trying them for the first time
at a tea room
in a salad
A miniature orange
I thought
Biting in to the whole
Feeling the tang
the almost-sour
surprise on my palette
followed by sweetness

Today I have a tree
in my front yard
under the window
Sweet blossom scent
wafts inwards
Biting into the harvest
the reality of both sensations
sweet and sour
taken in small measure
moments in a lifetime

Bittersweet

Mahima Gabriel – Wistful Wisteria

seeing Miss Wisteria
in only a weeks time
her winter leaves
now completely fallen

I'm right with her

life reflecting
falling leaves
questioning
will Spring
bloom once again

this year —

feeling
it can't come
SOON ENOUGH

we have many winters
in our lives
some only a few days
some for months or longer

This year —
too much winter

wistfully wishing
Spring will bloom
in me
with new colors

that spark JOY!

Len Germinara – No Thanks

Arturo somnambulated to the Mr. Coffee
as if his slippers bore him on a lazy Susan

On his 4th rotation past the island
he grabbed a cup
On the 5th he poured

 He skipped cream and sugar altogether
Certain the refrigerator and sugar bowl

Two bricks more than a full load

On the sixth spin of the cycle
he got off the merry go round

Joined his wife on the porch
where she sat rapt
two German Shepherds
                                    at her feet
                                            distance in her eyes

The coffee was weak
The last they had

            so   it had to do

As if a command had been uttered

both dogs stand up
with the last sip

Arturo and the wife rise as well
not a word between them

His mug in his right hand
she takes his left

The last morning
coming up over the Elk Mountains

                        Fireworks
                        Without sound

Andrew Laufer – See It Shimmer

There is much beauty to see
Attentive eyes will notice it everywhere
Few are present enough to witness it all the time

Beauty is   everywhere   all the time
Though we often don't see it
Unrecognized   unacknowledged

It comes into view   in precious moments
Rush to greet it   it is fleeting
Be aware   when it is hidden

With intention   seek it out
Absent strife   the world begins to sparkle
Practice peace   to see it shimmer

Nick LeForce – Everything Is A Poem

Everything is a poem.
If I say, "Today I stand still
while the world spins,"
then I have composed a lifetime.

The words can be like the everyday,
brushing your teeth, washing the kitchen counter,
confessing fruitless worries.

The sun will someday go dark
but until then be a moon that seeks for
and hides from the light.

There will always be a dark side:
the rash from stinging nettles,
the bitter nip of paper cut comments,
and the fear of neglected monsters
hiding in the closet.

These are poetry's playmates, too.

The quickest route to a shriveled heart
is trying to keep it from running
with the wrong crowd
settling, instead, for a half life.

Once you realize everything
is a poem, then you can say,
"This morning I woke up twice;
once when I rubbed the sleep
from my eyes, and once again
on the playground with playmates
all around."

Valerie Ries-Lerman – Challenge And Triumph

What you're given
> turn it around
> take another look
> what else can be found?

Create something new
> don't cling to the past
> you're born to create
> intelligence your path.

What you're given
> only a start
> you can transcend
> if you invite the spark.

Sharon Mahany – The Unforgettable Thing

lingered on his tongue each morning--
hoping to purge it with each rinse and spit.
This undesirable unforgettable thing

haunted his dreams each time he pillowed his head
day in and day out. It was the single most
important thing--the thing he forgot to remember.

Days were not counted like daisy petals,
plucked one at a time in slow playful gestures,
nor were they acknowledged for their beauty

like each stunning star in the sky.
Days were stepping stones to night;
Night, an odyssey to day.

Cycles of weeks and months wound round
like the precise metal gears of a clock,
clicking clacks of cogs and togs
moving through life with unforgettable speed.

Fear is like that—chasing people away from that
which they wish to forget. If they run fast enough
perhaps that thing will never catch up,
or perhaps they will forget all about
the thing in the running.

Reneé Marie – Wandering, Without An Earth

Earth was not unlike a perpetual toddler
pretending to be unaffected by the lack of
steady   thoughtful   parental supervision   often
wandering wildly oblivious   unharnessed   unprotected
also known to be powerful   vulnerable   adorable
spinning on her merry-go-round of innocence
hands-free in the whimsey of
just   being

I long to pinch her cheeky-typography
One   More   Time

Craving adoration   she sustained billions of parasites
even as her breath-taking beauty continued
to fracture and we with her   until
form-free in the ethers there
was no more willful denial
we sobbed and asked

what the hell
just   happened!

Mary McGrath – Why the Sea is Salt

My hand turned the crank and
now the sea is salt.
My hand dipped the thorn into poison
and pushed it into the apple.
Poor thing!

My own hand combed and
braided her hair, took my sharp
scissors and cut it off.
I held the braid on high and
dropped her man into brambles.

My hand put the cow up for sale
and threw the beans out the window.

My hand took off my skin as I
slipped out of the sea, and found it
again when my sisters rose out
of the calm.

My hand dropped white crumbs
into the dark forest floor,
with trees standing as spears
against sunlight.

My hand pushed the witch into
the oven where she joins
spiced and crumbling bodies.

It scatters seeds, shakes snowflakes
from the clouds, feasts on pages,
puts the book back on the shelf.

With no tears, no salty tears.

Esther Meyers – A Black-Blue Sky

A black-blue sky
Yellows and reds
A slumbering sea
Meeting misty heavens

We lift our gaze to a
Bowing Man of a Moon
Graced by the
Lovely Lady Venus

Mere moments before
The world had been ordinary
Beige and blue and green
Rocks and sky and trees

Now, a dark descent
On a rocky trail
An astonishing night
With a hand to hold

And there is fear
And there is danger
And there is magic
And there is love

Ann Privateer – A Lamp

Sits on my desk
Its hard unyielding
Surface shines

Its oval shape beckons
A gift so many years ago
I hardly remember

It lights the grayness
Makes everything
Readable without

Questioning
It's there for me
Waiting, listening

To do what I can't do.

Doreen Procope – Nature At Its Best

Dimensionless and immeasurable in boundless beauty
Unparalleled in creative artistry
Phenomenally majestic, the uniqueness of palleted wonder
Witness the amazingly fantastic sunset and sunrise

A delightful canopy of classic one hit wonder color diversification
Underscored is an overwhelming showcase of wonderment
No mere hand of man is able to capture this ever changing magic
Brought into existence by the mighty hand of God

The golden firmament intensifies in rich bold imagery
Continuously transformed by the winds of time
The atmospheric viability of might and collusion
Dance along the vivid rays of endless possibilities

What can rival such awesome hues of originality
Who can suffer the challenges of virginized imagination
Alas, we resign ourselves to the role of a willing spectator
As we witness the unfolding of incredible artistry

With eyes transfixed and mouths agape
Beholding the birth of this natural beauty
Sunrise and sunset represent nature at its best

Coast To Coast Poetry Consortium

Begun in June of 2021 the CCPC is a poetry critique group for active writers that convenes weekly, Sundays at 3:30 PST on Zoom. Facilitated by Len Germinara the group gives a cold reading of work submitted and a discussion afterwards with a five-minute maximum per poem. Space is limited, if interested in participation, contact Len Germinara at lensir@hotmail .com

Process and Format

The purpose of the group is to provide insight into the way your poetry is perceived on the printed page. A poem is presented in advance and sent to the facilitator who compiles a master document which is screen shared to the group. A member of the group is asked to read the poem aloud "cold". Once the piece is read a discussion ensues between the members of the group with the exception of the writer. The discussion is about the meaning, construction, and the overall impression of the piece. The writer is asked to listen without responding. This encourages a broad spectrum of insights into exactly what is working and what might require some adjustments. The discussion is always about the poem with not a thought or comment about the poet and what is known about them. The only requirement for participation is that each member of the group be working weekly on work that requires editing i.e., new work.

How To Access This Group

Interested writers can access this group through the Sacramento Poetry Center website: www.sacpoetrycenter.org

Len Germinara – www.lengerminara.com

Beth Bartel – My Lazy Days

My lazy days

are sparse   few   precious as gemstones

Most days are non-stop
with kids, work, obligations

So when a magical day of nothing arrives
I embrace it, milk it
I might not get this chance again for a while

Sipping coffee in bed
scrolling the Book of Faces
getting sucked down the TikTok rabbit hole
watching scary movies

Maybe I'll shower
maybe not
Maybe I'll get the mail
maybe not

I sure hope no one knocks on my door
They'd be unpleasantly surprised at what answers

Sure, the housework could use some catching up
but I purposely choose not to have purpose

It's an active choice to be a sloth

Stuart L. Canton – Carcinisation

Always there is that pulse, a kind of hum, radiating from the beginning, as when you stand in the river, and you shield your eyes from the sun, and for just a moment, you perceive the mountains, connecting that distant, icy origin with your cold toes, before a Frisbee brings you back to the earth, and the hum recedes, lost in the splashing as you step from the water, just like the muck beneath your calloused feet, crumbling mountains washing away...

But later, you'll look up at the red speck crossing the night sky, that iron, dust rock in the darkness, and in the silence it will seem you can hear humming radio waves beamed from the Mars rover, across 157 million miles, and maybe even the pulse of other things, older, and more final; and you'll puff and pass, or sip your whiskey, or you'll pull a blanket tighter around you, your breath hanging in the air. Whatever this moment is, there is the cold, and between the trees, the small red glow, and a robot on the other side of the chasm, scuttling between the rusted rocks of a long dead sea.

Diane Funston – Pieces

I collect fragments.
Old plates, odd earrings,
all imperfect puzzles to form a whole.

A ceramic mime, amethyst chunk,
clay snake, vintage marbles,
I hunt far and wide.

Yesterday, a saucer broke onto the floor, "Mosaic",
I said, gathered the shards with careful fingers,
put them in my box of crazy-quilt pottery.

I fit and cut and break and glue,
a different act than writing, no thinking
just pattern and instinct and color.

I leave them to bake in sun perfect for the task
I go inside, begin thinking under warm shower,
dress, then sit at desk and focus.

Move pen across paper, let words spill out,
poetic attempts to make sense of the world in language,
having used all the sharpest edges in pieces of broken glass.

Roger Funston – When I'm 85

I will walk the dogs on a late Fall Day
along a trail that follows a dry creek
through an oak woodland
A few yellow leaves clinging to bare branches
after the Fall color display
Snow veneer from recent storm lying along the creek bed
The sound of birds filling the air

I will walk in the late afternoon
Look down at mountain lion footprints in soft earth
Watch for bobcat moving through boulders
The sun sinking towards the horizon
Casting an orange glow on gray clouds

I will walk the land as seasons change
Delight in the hills greened by Spring snowstorms
Be lulled by the melody of flowing water in spring-fed creeks
Smell the dust and feel the warmth of summer days
Seek the cool shadows under oak canopy
Look in awe at Fall's burst of colors
Watch the silhouette of bare branches against a deep blue sky
Feel the briskness of Winter's chill

In the late Fall days of my life, I will
Take in the sights, sounds and smells while forest bathing
Seek out beauty in the world
Collect experiences, not things
Make the world a little better before I depart
Laugh, love, live because life is not a dress rehearsal
and there are no guarantees
But most of all...I will keep moving

Len Germinara – Benign Canid

3 feet proceeds me
most mornings

Leaves me scat
ghosts my track

Seldom seen more
than hind end

On purpose
I suppose

That he rarely
ranges far
or wide

leads me think someone
may be feeding him

The way 3 feet pees
indicates he's
she

moves well
in spite
the bum leg   she wanders on

What's the average
age
of a cape cod
coyote

I wonder

How many more
walks together
of a morning
will we have

Dennis Hock – Letting Go

For years, a door
has stood closed before me,
without comment.
It needs to be opened now.

Within, stairs lead downward.
They are neither steep nor shallow.
The light is natural.
There is no temperature.

As I descend,
the stairs keep unfolding underfoot.

I don't count the steps, for it
is not a question of depth
but of a compelling need to find out.
My initial anxiety has vanished.
Then, I realize, not even curiosity
is traveling with me anymore.

My head empty of thought and image,
I descend without agenda or anticipation.

There is nothing else to it.

Rachael Ikins – Flipping Channels

I heard a priest, tele-Mass today, say something
about light shining over all true believers, yeah,
but so much blood shed.
Why do many feel entitled to force their good idea on others?
Never mind. I smell coffee.

Yesterday, a small pod formed around a table,
honored the sacrificial pig and instant potatoes.
Two young men, their mother and me. No surprise, then,
Nancy's grass or when she spilled a wine portion
for the Old Ones a night last summer on my new porch:
we entered the world the same month.

Loss occupied other chairs. Later, brother urged brother
to tell about that relationship a few ago. No. Some closets
don't need reorganizing. Knowledge lay on the table
like a vernix-covered infant. Before the wailing,
someone comforted someone, and we laughed.

The dog shredded his own griefs, clouds strewn the carpet over.
Never speaks of his past. He takes medication.
Chemicals shrink anxiety to a side course, appetizer,
pale pink shrimp and ketchup you manage not to eat
without offending. Without making yourself sick.

My inner bedroom wall, mirror flip-sided,
Nancy's bedroom wall. Let's tin-can phone it,
I want to say. She prefers talk to text.

Gentleness offered kind hands to sleepers
who rested on their father's lap, lips still outlined
in brownie batter, eyelids sparkled a deep-lake turquoise.

Outside, clouds rained down, carried night in on their backs,
erased snow. I waded home through a canal. Time smells
like chocolate.

Angela J. James – A Tale Of 2 Pre-Schools

Buenos dias, children
Good morning, ninos
Buenos dias, teacher
Good morning, profesora
We all understand
we should speak softly, be kind
Mind la profesora, the teacher
We stand in line
we share crayons, we learn colors
Purple, pink, persimmon
the fruit only I have tasted
Laughter in English, in Spanish, in Spanglish
Tears in any language are fine
Speak softly, be kind, always mind

New school, new friends, new toys, new teacher
Buenos dias, profesora
Speak English, you're not Mexican

I know, I'm proudly peach
not red, not blue
but of indeterminable hue
reminiscent of exotic fruit
Only I have eaten

More letters, bigger numbers
Laugh, sing a piano song
Run, yell in the classroom
don't speak softly
Teacher doesn't mind
never says be kind

Andrew Laufer – Sixty-six and a Half

Exactly six months   until I'm 67
Mom has moved in   love having her here
She is frail   stays indoors now   too cold outside
Sits by the front picture window   feeling the warmth of the sun

I work outside   she can see me sometimes
Mowing the lawns   trimming the hedges   pulling   the weeds
Glancing at the window   I see her watching
I smile and wave   she smiles too waves back

Twenty-six years between us   ever my respected elder
Familial love   as natural as life itself   bolstered by her presence
Her acknowledgement   still soothing to my soul
Even at sixty-six and a half   the child within comes alive

Jameson Magdaleno – My Mother's Father

My mother's father was many things to me:
An occasional birthday card with a five-dollar bill
An 18-wheeler, CB handle, that didn't make detours
An empty seat at Papa's funeral
A yellowing picture of a young marine in dress blues
A '77 Monte Carlo with a souped up 454 big block and nitro
An old leather punching bag with all the air let out
A U.S. map with push pins in all the states
An old travel trailer with a gold tooth in a cabinet
A dozen worn-out baseball caps
A black pistol with a 30-round magazine
An old folding knife with worn-down blades in a dresser drawer
A pair of wire rimmed reading glasses
A brand-new Carhart jacket never worn
A genealogy report scrawled on a post-it note –
England 41%, Ireland 28%, Scandinavian 18%, W. Europe 12%, Fin./Rus.
1%
An empty prescription bottle of cancer meds
A 21-gun salute, Taps playing on a bugle, tri-fold American flag in a case
A funeral program on the refrigerator
A stack of bills and receipts on my mother's kitchen table
A toolchest, socket set, table vice, and shop stool in my garage
A picture of three-year-old me in an album
A welded cross on a mountain top in the Eastern Sierras
A memory that fades a little more each passing day

Sharon Mahany – As if They Had Wings

as if they had wings   **words**
move our hearts to flight
words leaf   from out the mouth
one green vein straining to petal
then another

strung   along

a tag-along

a little way

a long time

how we feel about our family
our friend's darn luck
a Movement across town

the internal movement   of idea
filaments of passion
brightened   once exposed to sunlight

within earshot
we feed on our own   **words**
often chew with mouth open
share a meal   with strangers

drop   a crisp feather
shriveled   unnourished
to make room for those   **words**
that potentially blossom
or better yet   take   flight

Conclusion

Experience is elusive. It is not something you can put in a box or hang on the wall. It's an inside job, a continuity of fleeting moments, wave after wave rolling onto the shore of our lives and then receding back into the inexpressible. We can try to describe our experience in words by pointing to the wrack zone, the remains left behind and marked by the high tide. We can do our best to paint a picture others might be able to see. But nothing brings us closer to the actual experience of wet sand under our feet or the taste of salty air in our mouths or the sound of the sea's cursive lettering on our ears or the rush and pull of waves on our bodies than poetry. Poetry is the language of experience. A good poem puts us there and can, in that moment, stand us on the ground we share no matter how far apart we live in space or time. A good poem is a companion of the heart because we realize we are not alone in our experience.

The beauty of an anthology is that it offers a wide selection of poetry from many different poets. With so many voices to express the inexpressible, we have more paths to the shore of our lives and more invitations to find and feel the common ground of experience we all share. Ideally, this Anthology of Sacramento Poetry Center Writing Groups will also provide more than enough inspiration for you to write or continue to write poetry yourself and to find companions of the heart in writing groups that encourage and support you on your journey through life. And if one of those groups happens to be with SPC, we welcome you!

Acknowledgments

This Anthology would not be possible without the commitment and dedication to writing of those who have joined in SPC writing groups over the years. Our writing groups thrive on the enthusiasm and willingness of new and seasoned poets. It is often a daunting step for writers to share their poetry and writing groups provide a safe place to share poems and get support and encouragement to develop as a writer. All who participated, whether they submitted a poem to the anthology or not, helped create the soil from which many of these poems sprouted. And, of course, we owe a special debt of gratitude to all the poets who contributed to the publication.

Our writing group facilitators, Len Germinara, Danyen Powell, Nick LeForce, and Bob Stanley deserve a special thanks for their work to create a safe, comfortable environment for writers to flourish. These groups meet weekly and the facilitators put in all the time and energy to make it happen without any compensation except the love of writing and sharing poetry and the rewards that come from engagement with a poetry community.

Finally, an applause goes out to the Sacramento Poetry Center board for sponsoring this project and especially to the current and former Board Members who served on the editorial committee: Angela James, Len Germinara, Ann Michaels, and Nick LeForce.

Contributors

Beth Bartel
Doreen Beyer
Maxine Boshes
Julie Hannah Brower
Stuart L. Canton
Vicki Carroll
Gene Cheever
Leslie Cummings
Sue Daly
Andru Defeye
Karen DeFoe
Susan Dlugach
M. J. Donovan
Diane Funston
Roger Funston
Mahima Gabriel
Len Germinara
Nancy Ginsberg
Joan Goodreau
Tom Hedt
Dennis Hock
Rachael Ikins
Angela J. James
Gary Kruse

Nick LeForce
James Magdaleno
Sharon Mahany
Reneé Marie
Laura Martin
Mary McGrath
Esther Meyers
Ann Michaels
Matthew Mitchell
Shawn Pittard
Betsy (Sunderland) Powell
Danyen Powell
Marilynn Price
Ann Privateer
Doreen Procope
David Quinley
Kris Robinson
Valerie Ries-Lerman
Laura Rosenthal
Allegra Jostad Silberstein
Bob Stanley
Patricia Wentzel
Susan Wolbarst
Arlene Downing-Yaconelli

SPC Editorial Staff:

Len Germinara
Ann Michaels

Angela J. James
Nick LeForce

For information about The Sacramento Poetry Center,
please visit our website: sacpoetrycenter.org

Made in the USA
Middletown, DE
27 May 2023